ALLEN PHOTO...

SHOWING IN HAND

CONTENTS

PREPARATION AT HOME

The preparation of the in-hand animal begins at home. The show ring is not the place to begin educating a youngster because once in the ring the animal's attention will be absorbed by the sights and sounds surrounding him.

Start with your youngster as soon as possible, getting him used to being tied up in the stable, having his feet picked out, his legs touched, being groomed and having rugs on etc.

By using a variety of people around your youngster, who could also wear various hats, coats etc., you can simulate judges and stewards in the ring. At some shows, youngstock are measured so it is important that he is used to strangers approaching him with a measuring stick.

This general handling will make tasks such as plaiting, loading and schooling much easier later on.

AUTHOR'S TIP

When teaching youngsters to load and unload, they should be discouraged from jumping up or down the ramp of the horsebox and encouraged to walk quietly instead. Foals seem particularly inclined to do this when unloading and can easily hurt themselves. It is better, therefore, to cradle them and, if necessary, lift them out.

SCHOOLING

Treat each animal as an individual rather than trying to produce them all in the same way.

Firstly, it is important that the youngster learns to walk forward as naturally as possible alongside the handler, neither hanging back nor shooting forward resembling a badly trained Great Dane. The former can be rectified by employing the help of an assistant to send him on from behind or, if you are on your own, using a long whip (in your left hand) to tap him on the quarters, taking care that he does not twist his quarters away from you.

To keep the in-hand animal as straight as possible, walking alongside a hedge or fence will help, as will leading him from the offside. The latter is necessary as all in-hand showing is performed on the right rein with the animal led on the nearside and this often results in him becoming one-sided. Apart from providing a little variety in his schooling regime this will also help to prevent him from learning to turn his head toward you and swing his quarters away from you – a common occurrence in the ring.

When working on the trot, find the animal's natural rhythm and, above all, keep it steady with you in control having a light but firm contact. Remember that a pony or horse will copy the handler's stride (*see below*) and it is important, therefore, for you to trot slowly and with as long a stride as you can. If your charge is an outstanding mover he will usually be happier flowing along more than the bad mover who will need to be kept in check more.

Practise at first in a school or small field and then vary it by going into a larger open space, or up and down hills which will also have the advantage of improving the animal's muscle tone whilst at the same time giving him a change of scenery.

Finally, teach him to halt in balance because, as with the ridden animal, the in-hand exhibit is at rest for most of the class. Your youngster should also learn to put his feet back squarely when the judge has picked them up.

LUNGEING

The main question with lungeing is when to start. A little lungeing particularly at the beginning of the season, teaches the animal to work on a circle, which can improve right bend and correct crookedness. Lungeing will also improve movement, balance and outline.

If your animal will settle just walking around the showground, then lungeing is unnecessary, however if he becomes excitable then it may be beneficial at a show, providing he has been well taught at home.

Side reins may be used in extreme cases, particularly to correct a fault: one on the offside could help improve bend, for example. They must only be used as a guide, never to force the head carriage, and must have an elastic insert to allow a certain amount of give.

Some people prefer to long-rein rather than lunge believing that this teaches the animal to go forward more into his bridle on a straight line and, therefore, he is less likely to become one-sided.

SHAPES

It is essential that the overall picture of the in-hand animal is regularly monitored. The shape of youngstock in particular can change rapidly as they grow, i.e. they become leggy or appear higher behind etc. Broodmares may need extra feeding to compensate for the foal inside as well as the foal at foot both of which will take condition from her.

Show broodmares should be exactly that, (*see top picture*) they should not look like old, saggy paddock mares nor ridden show horses or ponies which happen to have a foal alongside. A novice broodmare, however, will get away with looking a bit lighter than her more experienced counterpart.

A yearling with a nice 'rainbow' front, i.e. a good turn of front, must look like a yearling and not a three-year-old, or older. These days, judges are a lot more aware of the dangers of encouraging exhibitors to over-produce youngstock and sometimes discourage them by placing them down the line. An overweight animal will have an extra burden on his limbs which, particularly in the younger ones, could result in splints, windgalls etc.

TACK

BRIDLES

Youngstock may be shown in either a leather show headcollar or snaffle bridle. Yearlings are usually shown without bits unless they are colts or particularly head-strong. Stallions and colts aged two years or over must always be shown bitted. I have seen many three-year-olds shown in snaffle bridles, and sometimes, in the case of hunters, a double bridle, which makes them appear more of a positive prospect for ridden classes. However, the handler should always have the ability to keep control without resorting to overbitting.

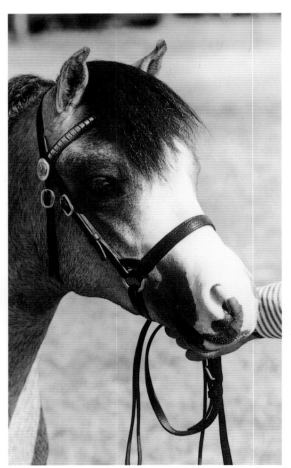

AUTHOR'S TIP

Rather than holding double reins as one, dividing them with your forefinger gives you more control over the animal's direction.

Broodmares may be shown in a leather show bridle or snaffle, double or pelham bridle depending on which they are happiest in. If they like the pelham, then a slip-head may be used for cosmetic purposes to make a plain head appear less bare. Foals are usually shown in foal slips or special show bridles and must not be bitted under National Pony Society Rules. It is better to have a good quality, adjustable bridle on foals as their heads can alter enormously throughout the show season. Those with cheek pieces fixed onto the noseband are better than those which slide around the noseband and could rub against the animal's eye (*see right*). Throatlatches which are part of the head piece are much better than those which are separate and only joined at the poll, which can easily trap hair around the ears.

Many native ponies are shown in webbing and rope halters which give a more workmanlike look in keeping with their role. Arabs, however, can be shown in the special, very fine Arab bridles which have rolled leather and enhance the classic outline of the head, but they must be strong enough to contain the animal as many Arab shows will fine you if your animal gets free!

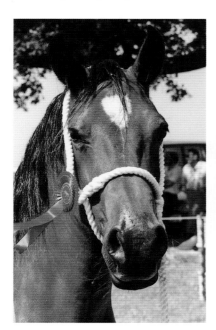

Your bridle for the in-hand class must be in good repair and fit the animal well thus enhancing the overall picture as well as being secure enough to be safe. Loose, flapping cheek pieces may frighten the animal as well as, possibly, coming undone, these should also be even on both sides and fully adjustable to ensure the best fit.

A common problem with bridles is the thickness of the leather: too fine and the animal will look bare, possibly plain, too thick and you will lose a pretty head in it. Try different styles of bridle to find which is best. All brass fitments must be well polished. Browbands must fit well: a tight one will make the animal uncomfortable as well as making his forehead seem very bare, whereas a slack one will look untidy. Mares' and foals' browbands usually co-ordinate.

BITS

There is no hard-and-fast rule for bits, and experimentation at home, not on the show-ground, is your best policy. They should fit properly in the mouth as any tightness or rubbing will make the pony very uncom-fortable and will lead to problems when he is ridden. Having your bit too low will only cause more problems as the animal can learn to put his tongue over the bit. Some handlers prefer straight bar bits, whereas others like jointed bits. They can be rubber, vulcanite or metal and may be wrapped in chamois or similar material if required. One leading exhibitor soaks the material on the bit in glycerin and rubs it along the bars of the mouth to encourage youngsters to salivate. Bitting is an extremely important part of your animal's education and if badly done will cause many problems in the future.

LEAD REINS

Lead-rein lengths vary considerably and it is important that you select the correct length and thickness for your animal. Too long and not only will you be carrying yards of excess rein in your hand but also you could be tempted to give the animal too much rein. Too short and you will not be able to show him off properly as he will feel constrained, especially if he takes fright or lunges forward. When in the ring always keep an eye out for the animal chewing his rein as, obviously, it could break.

With lead reins and attachments, it, again, all boils down to personal preference and what suits the individual animal. The lead rein can be attached directly to the noseband to save the youngster's mouth or, with the help of a coupling, go directly onto the mouth ensuring an even pressure (*right*). Alternatively, you can use the coupling and noseband together for more control adopting the best of both variations (*far right*).

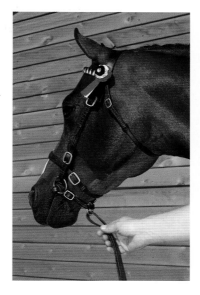 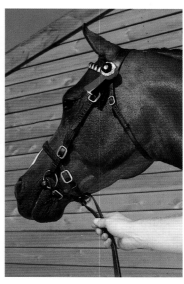

Another way of attaching the lead rein is to fasten it onto the nearside of the bit and thread it through to the offside (*below left*) which will help to stop the animal bending around you and also encourages it to bend right around the corners. For extra control on a colt which is a handful, a rein with a chain can be used in a similar way (*below*).

 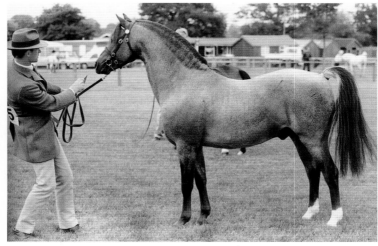

If using the rein conventionally, I prefer a plain leather lead rein to the chain variety as the chain can slip through your hand. The rein with a buckle attachment is far more secure than that with a clip which can come undone quite easily. Make sure that the tongue of the buckle has not become sharp and pointed as any sudden tugs by the exhibit could pull the buckle through your hand and cause a nasty cut especially if you are not wearing gloves. If you do use a lead rein with a clip, remember that it must always fasten away from the animal so that it doesn't pinch or become embedded in the skin.

DRESS

There is a more relaxed dress code in the in-hand world, although looking scruffy in dirty jeans and a tee-shirt is going to detract from the overall picture which would seem a pointless exercise. The best idea is to watch the classes you intend to compete in to see what is acceptable, whether it be suits and bowlers, tweed jackets, slacks and caps or trilbys, or, when showing Arabs, you need to be predominantly in white. It is certainly hard work on a summer's day running about with in-hand exhibits and I usually wear a blazer rather than a tweed jacket.

Most people wear shirts and ties; do make sure in the case of the latter that they are fastened down and will not flap about during your individual show, possibly frightening your animal.

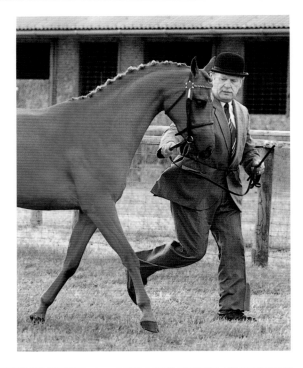

Some people cannot be bothered with hats either because they may be blown off in windy conditions or can be knocked off by an unruly colt. However, for this reason it may be practical to wear a riding hat to afford you some protection from flying hooves. For the most part though many would feel improperly dressed without some sort of headgear and some judges may expect it.

Suitable footwear is an important item of your clothing which can often be over-looked. You need to be able to run comfort-ably and not slip on the 'bowling green' surfaces common during the summer months or alternatively sink into inches of mud. Lace-ups are best but make sure the laces are secure and cannot come undone.

Gloves are not only correct dress but are vital when leading anything as they will protect you from nipping youngsters, burns if the animal pulls away sharply and also help to keep a grip on the rein in bad weather. In the latter case you may prefer to wear the nylon pimpled gloves.

It is useful to carry a showing cane (check with the relevant societies regarding the permitted length) as opposed to a dressage whip, to stop the animal falling in to you and to discipline naughty animals from the outset.

For finals and bigger competitions, in-hand exhibitors can wear smarter clothes; mare and foal handlers look much better with matching outfits. If grooms need to come into the ring with rugs and waterproofs on a cold, wet day then they should be smartly turned out as well.

AUTHOR'S TIP

Check before you enter the ring that you have any relevant cards for special awards and rosettes etc. (and a measuring slip if required) safely in your jacket pocket.

IN THE RING

Using your common sense pays dividends, assess the competition before entering the ring and try to place your animal behind and, if possible, in front of lesser ones in order to make your own look better.

MANNERS

Although manners are not of paramount importance to the in-hand judge, you must have your animal settled for the ring so that he can give a good account of himself. Usually judges will penalise bad behaviour if they feel that they cannot judge the animal as a consequence of it or that the animal constitutes a danger in the ring. If you are showing a colt or stallion in a mixed class or championship, then it pays to keep him as far away as possible from any fillies in the line up.

GAITS

When showing an animal with a good walk, avoid being held up behind a shorter striding one which will mean that you will not be able to show him to his best advan-tage. The walk must be free and even with the animal going forward and tracking-up well, he must go into his bridle and be light in the hand with the handler doing the minimum of work. This also applies to the trot, when the animal should always look straight ahead and maintain a steady and relaxed head carriage.

> **AUTHOR'S TIP**
>
> Many exhibitors forget about matching the handler to an animal. A very tall person will make a youngster, especially a foal, look much smaller, and vice versa, and the whole picture could, therefore, be less eyecatching.

The transitions to and from walk, trot and halt should be smooth and precise in order to give fluency to your performance as, unlike the ridden animal, you have less scope for impressing the judge.

When performing your initial trot, walk the first few strides to settle and balance your animal before quietly going into trot. Once the gait is established, move up a

> **AUTHOR'S TIP**
>
> So many handlers fly off into a fast trot resulting in the animal breaking into canter, which gives an untidy overall impression. If this happens during the show, come back to trot immediately. However, if it happens during the initial trot out and shortens your display, then once back in trot continue your display past the others instead of going straight back into your place.

gear along the front, giving your show a more professional look remembering to keep the rhythm flowing especially around the corners, by using your right hand to guide the head round. Be confident and look ahead so that you can find the best line to make full use of the ring and at the same time avoid the animal falling in toward the judge. Your transition back to walk should be precise giving a polished ending to the exercise, not crashing into the animal in front like a runaway train!

Try to keep the animal standing up well at all times in the ring as you never know when the judge may cast a comparing eye over the line up.

BROODMARES AND FOALS

Although in theory former ridden mares are generally easier to show in hand as they are more accustomed to show procedure, in practice their foal could be a distraction, particularly with a novice mare who will be 'foal proud' at the beginning.

A strategically placed foal is vital when showing a mare and vice versa: it can make or break an impressive display. Even the best laid plans may need adapting once in the ring, however, which is why the handlers of both mare and foal have to work as a partnership and in some cases be almost telepathic to cope with unexpected situations!

Generally, the foal should accompany the mare most of the time: behind her, alongside her on the outside or in front of her if she needs to see where it is. Neither the mare nor foal should ever be in a position to obstruct the judge's view of the other.

Before performing the initial trot out, the foal handler will usually take the foal to the other end of the ring so that the mare can see it as she does her display. However, if the mare begins to panic on realising that the foal is no longer at her side, you will have to change your plans and meet the mare halfway along the long side or return back to the mare and keep with her whilst trotting.

With one or two exceptions, foals show better with their dams nearby. If required to perform an initial trot out, keeping the mare in exactly the right place to ensure that the foal strides out is an art in itself (*see below*). By going too far in front with the mare, the foal is likely to leap into canter to catch up with her whereas too far behind and it will probably stop dead in its tracks.

As with the youngster, let your foal find a rhythm in trot before running on. If it does break into canter, warn the mare handler to hold back to encourage it to come back into trot.

As foals like to see other foals, try to get one in view as an encouragement to yours to walk on, particularly if you are in the lead, otherwise it might hang back. Obviously foals are not expected to be 'foot perfect' but if well presented they will be successful. Do not neglect the role of the foal when showing a broodmare as judges will often compare foals when assessing their dams. If your mare is without a foal for whatever reason she may therefore be at a disadvantage when assessed with another mare of equal merit with a foal.

AUTHOR'S TIP

Although a showing cane is handy when leading a youngster, especially if it strikes out, be careful that the cane does not frighten it and make it retreat. Letting the animal chew the end of your cane is also quite dangerous as the cane could splinter in the mouth and cause damage. Similarly, flapping rosettes around the handler's waist might also spook the animal.

AUTHOR'S TIP

Do not allow lead reins on foals and youngsters to get too long because you risk a foot getting caught in the loop. If this does happen, catch hold of the rein near the animal's head and pull the spare end through gently to avoid panicking it.

THE IN-HAND SHOW

STANDING UP

Once in line, work out where the best ground is to stand your animal up – avoid rough ground – so that you can come out of line and straight into the right place in a professional manner and face the direction in which you intend to walk away; look out for show jumps and other obstacles which would get in the way of your show.

Always stand the animal on the level or slightly uphill; downhill will make him look terrible and if he is higher behind than in front, this will be highlighted.

Once in front of the judge, stand the animal up with all four legs visible and the hind leg nearest the judge slightly behind the other. As the judge moves round to the other side either move the animal forward or backwards to reverse the hind leg position. Make sure that he stands straight so that when viewed from behind or in front the legs are square. Knowing how to correct a bad stance with your particular animal is very important as some are better pushed back a stride and others better pulled forward. Practise at home so that you will be more efficient in the ring and not keep the judge waiting.

The correct positioning of the head and neck is also important; if he is lacking in length of rein or has a cresty neck then stretching his front will give more quality and length to the picture. If he has a weak top line and is muscled under his neck you must keep him low and try to get an arch in the neck.

Common mistakes include:

1. having the animal's legs too spread out;

2. the head carriage too high;

3. and 4. the head turned, thus shortening the animal's front;

5. the handler obstructing the judge's view.

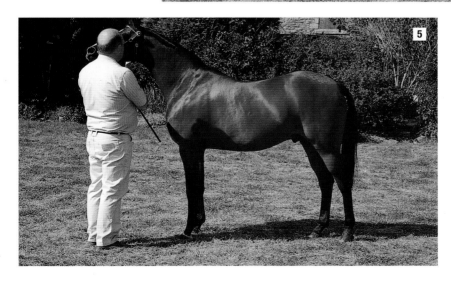

Keep some crackly paper or something that he will find interesting in your pocket to keep him amused so that, hopefully, he will stand still. Do be careful, however, when giving nuts or mints to an animal in the ring – they quickly become accustomed to getting treats and then start to demand them often resulting in nipping and, in the worst cases, temper tantrums. If you have to pick a little grass to keep him interested then take particular care when bending down that the animal doesn't strike out or move and spoil his stance.

When standing foals up, the main aim is to keep them occupied and looking alert which often involves a lot of coaxing rather than bullying.

THE INDIVIDUAL SHOW

When you walk away from the judge keep on a straight line (focusing on an object such as a particular trade stand or flag etc., will help to keep you on a good line) and in an even rhythm. As you reach the end of your walk turn slightly off your track to the left and then perform a half circle (with you on the outside) so that you end up on the same line that you took in walk. The animal should stay up into his bridle and the turn be big enough for him not to catch or twist himself. As you return to the same line, walk a couple of strides to compose the animal and commence your trot gradually building up to a free, rhythmic gait so that the judge can see if your animal moves straight.

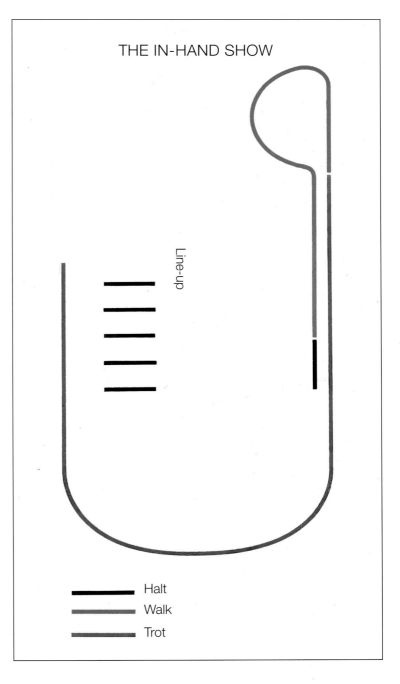

THE IN-HAND SHOW

Line-up

Halt
Walk
Trot

AUTHOR'S TIP

A common mistake is to start trotting before you are on a straight line, i.e. on a turn, which may make the animal catch himself and become lame. Some people deliberately avoid trotting a straight line to the judge if their animal does not move straight. However if the judge cannot see the animal move he cannot judge him and you would, therefore, probably be penalised for this. Also animals are often trotted too fast which results in them becoming unbalanced and sometimes going unlevel. This also results in plaiting or dishing which makes the animal look much worse.

As you trot past the judge continue around the back of the line-up in case he is still watching.

When showing broodmares, make sure that the foal does not interrupt the judge's view of her during her individual show. If she is foal proud it is better to have the foal directly in front of her, then she will concentrate instead of worrying and becoming unsettled, and when you do your show keep the foal with her.

Normally the foal would be standing in front and slightly away from the mare to make her look interested. Keep the foal in the same place while the mare walks away

from the judge and start to trot the foal as she trots back so that the foal will almost be giving her a lead.

After the mares have been judged, foals are more often than not pulled forward in a line in front of their mothers to be assessed either before going round as a class or doing their individual shows followed by a final walk round.

When performing the individual show with a foal the procedure is the same as with the mare but, obviously, the roles are reversed.

AUTHOR'S TIP

Some foals look very smart plaited and this usually works well with the more mature ones. Obviously those that are weak in appearance will be far better with their manes waterbrushed over to the offside instead. However, you might find that by the middle of the season they have matured enough to be plaited with high plaits. Plait to improve the picture, not just for the sake of it; putting five chunky plaits in is not going to improve a foal's appearance and may even make it look worse. The decision whether or not to plait a foal's tail depends on the individual; some foals go tense behind because of it, particularly if it is done too tightly. Normally foals' tails are plaited even if their manes are not.

ACKNOWLEDGEMENTS

I would like to thank Penny Hollings for her help in preparing this book.

I would also like to thank the photographers:
John Minoprio of Town and Country Productions Ltd. who supplied the photographs taken at Blue Slate Stables, kindly sponsored by Claire Francis of Pretty Ponies; Chris Cook of Pleasure Prints Area D and Cherry Wilde of Pleasure Prints Area K who supplied photographs taken in the show ring.

© J.A. Allen & Co. Ltd 1997
First published in Great Britain 1997
Reprinted 2009

ISBN 978-0-85131-677-2

J.A. Allen
Clerkenwell House
Clerkenwell Green
London EC1R 0HT

J.A. Allen is an imprint of Robert Hale Limited

www.halebooks.com

No part of this book may be reproduced, stored in a retrieval system, or transmitted, in any form or by any means, electronic, mechanical, photocopying, recording or otherwise, without the prior permission of the publisher. All rights reserved.

British Library Cataloguing-in-Publication Data.
A catalogue record for this book is available from the British Library

Design and typesetting by Paul Saunders
Series editor, Jane Lake
Printed in China by Midas Printing International Limited